Our Light

A story about a pandemic baby

by Monique E. Simões

To my pandemic baby, Matteo.
We love you – Mommy, Daddy, A & J

Let me tell you a story
about the time when you were born.

There was a virus going around
and masks were to be worn.

We were a bit worried and unsure

of what was happening in the world.

But we felt comfort

when inside mommy's belly you twirled.

Each day the news exploded
with information.

We held each other tight
trying to understand the situation.

Off to appointments mommy went
with a mask on her face.

She rubbed her belly twice
knowing you are in a safe place.

Several times everything had to shut down.

But with you coming soon, it was hard to frown.

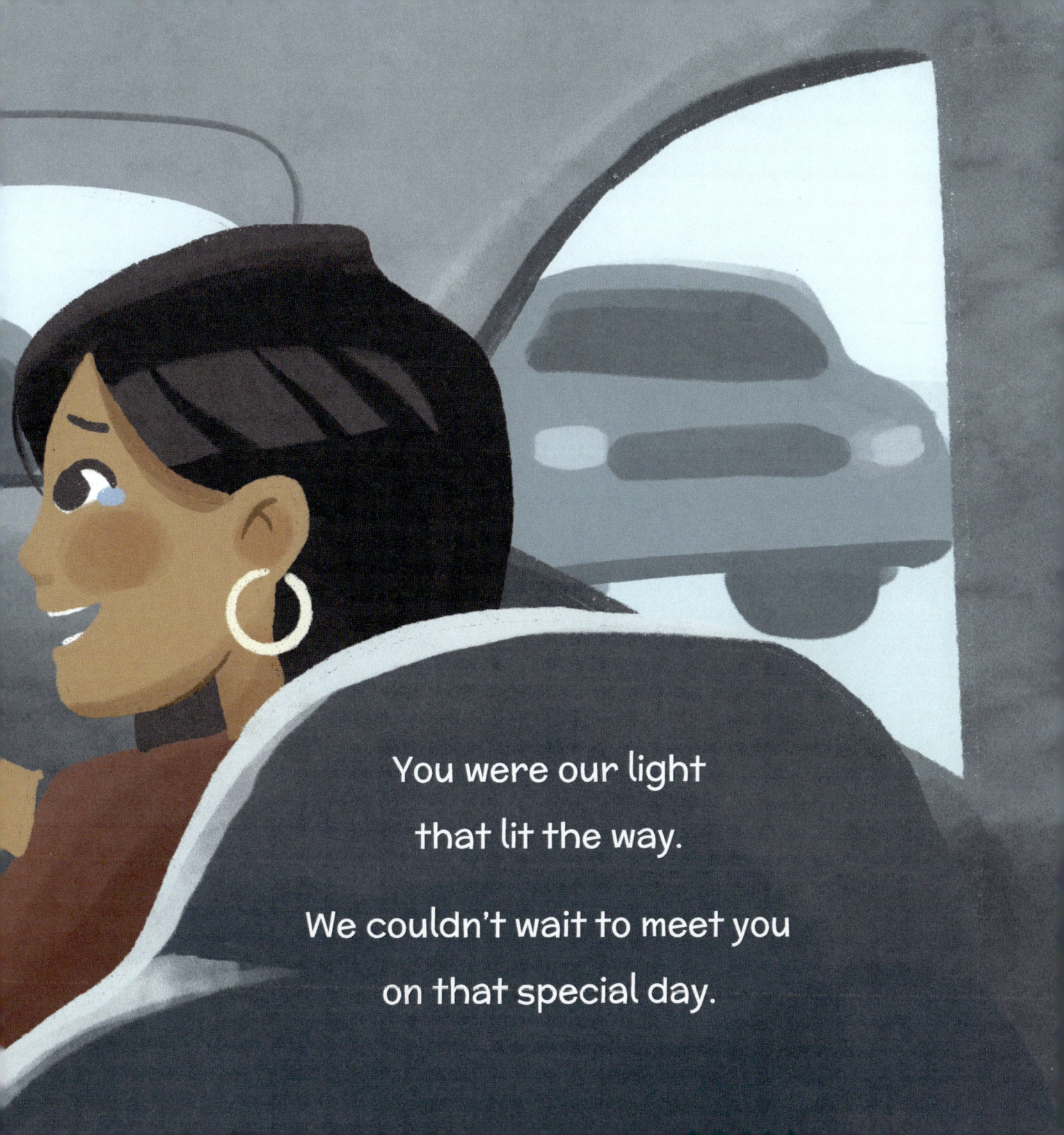

You were our light
that lit the way.

We couldn't wait to meet you
on that special day.

And when you arrived

it filled our hearts and all its spaces.

And for a moment we forgot the virus

that made us wear masks on our faces.

When the time came to bring you home...

No one could come visit, we had to stay alone.

This certainly was not
what we had imagined.

But during this time is
when special bonding happened.

Covid-19 tried to

make our lives real tough.

And though it was at times,

seeing your face made things less rough.

You were our light every single day.

Getting us through each month
in your own special way.

"Pandemic baby" is what some may call you.
But to us you're the light that kept shining through.

We love you. Keep shining.

Manufactured by Amazon.ca
Bolton, ON